Contents

This book is dedicated to Colleen Collins Smith and Genevieve Gudde

Acknowledgments:

Judy Bare
Sherri Downes
Kathleen Yoakum
Kit Carpenter

It is surprising that a book like The Dancer Prepares
*has not been written before. It is an absolute
necessity. It should be a prerequisite to any technique
class or, better still, required reading before any
student could claim to have committed himself to the long,
arduous course of study required by dance.*

In The Dancer Prepares, *James Penrod and Janice Gudde
Plastino have explained many things with remarkable
simplicity, and the knowledge they provide can save
immeasurable time in the classroom. Although it
is written primarily for those studying modern dance,
the book will help teachers of all types of dance.*

*This book is an invaluable contribution to the body
of educational dance literature.*

EUGENE LORING

THE *Dancer Prepares*

MODERN DANCE for BEGINNERS

JAMES PENROD
University of California, Irvine

JANICE GUDDE PLASTINO
University of California, Irvine

Illustrations   Robert Carr

MAYFIELD PUBLISHING COMPANY
285 Hamilton Avenue, Palo Alto, California 94301

GV
1783
.P44
1970

Copyright © 1970 by the National Press

Third Printing

Library of Congress Catalog Card Number: 79-101528
Standard Book Number: 87484-136-4
Manufactured in the United States of America

Preface

This book is written for you who are taking your first course in modern dance to introduce you to the content of the course and to explain your role as a student. It is assumed you have little or no background in the art or technique of the dance.

No one can be taught how to be an artist, but he can be taught the craft of an art form. We hope to help you discover a new appreciation of the arts in general and to inspire in you a desire for self-discovery, self-discipline, and eventually self-expression in the art form of dance. This book introduces you to such rudiments of the dancer's craft as basic techniques, dance clothes, and the care of your body. It also discusses choreographic fundamentals and evaluation procedures. We hope these objective principles will help you to form a subjective ideal which will inspire you to commit yourself more fully to the dance world.

It is of little consequence why you have decided to study modern dance. The important thing is that you have enrolled in a course to learn the most exciting of the movement forms. We do not assume that you will become a professional dancer, although we have directed the ideas in this book toward that goal. We do, however, hope you will experience the joy of movement well-executed, the exhilaration of creative endeavor, and the appreciation of dance—the most fleeting of the art forms.

Although the book is primarily concerned with the analysis of modern dance techniques, combinations, and vocabulary, some principles of ballet technique are included to show the interrelationship of all dance forms. The book, while written for the beginning student, contains information that will be of value to the intermediate student as well.

You have chosen a course that is physically rigorous and exhausting, mentally stimulating and exasperating, and creatively exciting and frustrating. It is probably one of the most self-satisfying courses that you will take.

We do not intend to preach a philosophy or theory of some ephemeral art form that can be mastered by meaningless statements about how to dance. We do intend to deal with concrete, specific, practical matters relating to the mastery of the creative and technical aspects of dance. v

"Love the Art in Yourself, not Yourself in the Art."
—Stanislavsky

Values

If you have signed up for your first modern dance class, which might be called something like Modern, Contemporary, Creative, Freestyle, Dance 40A, or PE 5B, you may be wondering just what modern dance is.

DEFINING MODERN DANCE

In the past, "modern dance" represented the viewpoints and movement concepts of each of several dancers or choreographers. For example, there was the particular modern dance technique of Martha Graham, of Doris Humphrey, and of Mary Wigman. As the horizons of the dance artists have widened, the various movement forms have become more alike. In the past, it was easy to recognize ballet by its codified positions and movements. This is no longer true. Today many "ballet" choreographers utilize the movement concepts of the modern dancer, and many of the body placements and exercises of the ballet dancer are now used in the "modern" techniques. Many choreographers now include in their work not only the elusive modern dance techniques, but also the principles of jazz, ballet, and ethnic dance.

A Blend of Techniques

If the term "modern dance" were to be defined for today, it should be broad enough to include all the diverse approaches existing now and likely to exist in the future.

Rather than a concise definition of what modern dance is, perhaps more important to you is what it can contribute to the enrichment of your life. It can help keep your body trim, give a grace and poise to all your movements, and contribute to your general sense of well-being through the pleasure of a well-toned body. It can introduce you to a new form in which you experience the joy of movement

What Dance Can Do for You

1

and compete solely with yourself. It can heighten your appreciation of music, the plastic arts, and all movement forms. It can increase your respect and understanding of the dancer's profession. And, finally, a modern dance course will expand your awareness and appreciation of the way you and others move.

DANCE AS A CAREER

It is hoped that some of you will be inspired enough by your modern dance experience to choose dance as a professional career. Dedication to the art of the dance *might* require you to forsake money, fame, and even family in order to reach the pinnacle of artistic success in the dance world. Many sacrifices are involved in such an aspiration, often without the longed-for rewards. After five to ten years of dedicated work, you may not yet be accepted into a dance company. Even if you are accepted, the company may be unable to pay you a living wage. You must often be prepared to support yourself by means other than dancing. Because the financial rewards are so low, living conditions may be barely adequate and certainly not luxurious. The hardships of giving concerts or arranging performances of your own works can be heartbreaking as well as rewarding.

Yet under such trying circumstances the art of dance flourishes. Dedicated, disciplined people continue to expand the vocabulary of movement. New forms are continually created in the artist's push forward. The hope of making a contribution to the understanding of life keeps the search alive. This is their reward.

Perhaps dance does not appeal to you on that level. Perhaps you have seen the beautiful women and handsome men, dressed in the latest fashions, who dance across television or movie screens. Such "Hollywood dreams" are within the realm of possibility. But you must decide whether you are willing to make the commitment necessary to attain them.

There have been and will continue to be those few dancers who have extraordinary luck and who obtain a good job without too much hard work. This happens rarely and in the long run usually has disastrous results. Almost always, these dancers fail because an inadequate background and bad training have not prepared them for the next job. It is risky to let yourself be talked into a job before you are ready. If your training is to be interrupted or stopped by a job, then think twice before you take that job.

Performing experience should be a part of your dance education, but it should supplement training, not take the place of it.

Anyone who does decide to dedicate himself to a dance career must be prepared to work, and work hard. He may perform before he has had five years of training, but he must continue to return to the classroom to keep his body in top condition. The dancer's body is his working instrument, as a violin is a violinist's instrument. Unlike the violinist, however, the dancer must build his instrument at the same time that he is learning technique and the skills needed to perform.

But a dancer's goal should be like that of the Olympic athlete, who dedicates himself to acquiring the greatest skills possible—not for financial gain or simply to win, but for the satisfaction of giving the best that is in him. No less than a devoted athlete, the dancer must discipline and dedicate himself to such a high purpose.

DANCE FOR VIEWING

As a dance student, you should attend dance concerts to see the finished product which was started in the studio. It is often impossible to see a professional performance unless you are living in a large city or near a large university specializing in dance. The alternative is to see professional performances on film and television. Many excellent films of dance exist and can be ordered for a small fee. Commercial television seldom offers first-rate concert dance, but it does offer entertaining dance by exciting, competent performers and choreographers. Educational television often shows new works as well as films of older works of leading choreographers. Many universities have fine companies or Orchesis groups—Orchesis is a national collegiate dance group with individual chapters on a number of campuses—who do exciting, creative productions. It is to your advantage as a student to see dance, whether good or bad. You can always learn something at a dance concert, even if it is something not to do.

Dance Audiences

The audience for modern dance is regrettably small. There are several reasons for this. One is that modern dance is a relatively new art and is not yet a socially "in" activity. As opposed to opera and ballet, which are often supported financially by an established society, modern dance is thought by many people to be only for other artists and dancers. This is unfortunate. Modern dance reflects the time in which it is danced. It is usually contemporary, because it is created by and for those who are interested in the reflection of life today.

Another reason modern dance has not enjoyed a wide following in the past is the stigma which existed upon using the human body as a medium for art. The Puritan influence fostered the belief that the sinful body should be hidden from view; only the mind and soul were worthy of serious study. More recently, the human body has become more acceptable as an appropriate medium for artistic expression. The belief that dancing bodies are sinful now exists only in certain sections of our society, and even there this view happily is undergoing some change.

Audiences and Finances

Many modern dance artists and their companies are beginning to enjoy limited financial support as they become acceptable to the general public. One artist who has done a great deal to promote the acceptance of modern dance is Martha Graham. Her success has come slowly, only after many years of work and dedication.

But even such famous artists as Martha Graham cannot maintain their companies on audience support alone. Most of the established professional companies are forced to rely on private foundation money or government grants. As with other gifts of funds, certain stipulations are frequently imposed on the person who accepts them. These demands may hinder or help the artist. It would be to everybody's advantage if the companies could be supported by the audiences who attend the performances.

Certainly the size of an audience is not always the best measure of the quality of a work of art. Artists are often ahead of their times. One criterion of the caliber of the artist is his ability to see new trends and to synthesize his insights in a new way. Therefore works of art may not evoke a response from the majority of people, who have not been introduced to the situation as the artist has interpreted it.

Like the centuries of dancers who have gone before, you are embarking on one of the most exciting experiences of a lifetime. Even if your dance training consists of one course only, the movements you will do can awaken you to an unlimited range of body movements. You will dance about those things that concern all men everywhere. These things are the search for an awareness of what it means to be alive, to create, and to begin to understand man and his place in the universe.

"The human body is an instrument for the production of art in the life of the human soul."
　　　　　　　—Alfred North Whitehead

CHAPTER 2

Preparation

After signing for a modern dance class, you might be asking yourself—as many students do—a series of questions. What should I wear? How should I wear it? What happens in a dance class? How much do I need to know about music? All are good questions, and the answers will help you get the most out of your classroom experience.

This chapter provides general answers. To learn the special requirements of your course, check with your teacher or a representative of the class. Some teachers like to use the first class meeting as a discussion period, and so you should find out whether ordinary clothes or dance clothes should be worn to the first session. If there are any unanswered questions in your mind, ask! Most teachers are used to answering questions and are happy to help.

CLOTHING
Special
Requirements

Often the beginning dance student wonders why in most dance studios he is asked to wear special form-fitting clothing for the dance class, clothing that could be thought of as an outer skin. There are several reasons.

Dance is a visual art that uses the dancer's body to create architectural designs in space. Any clothing that does not conform to the outline of his body will alter the designs created in that space. Some students might ask if this isn't desirable in some cases. The answer would be an emphatic Yes. Clothing can evoke an era, enhance some movements, and give a new look to the movement and the spatial design that a silhouetted body alone could never achieve. Students in a basic technique class, however, are

5

not usually concerned with these problems, unless they are experimenting to find new movements inherent in the restrictions imposed by the costume.

The second reason for special clothing is that the main concern of classroom technique is to align your body in a series of exercises that will strengthen and stretch it in order to make it responsive to the physical demands that will be made upon it. The teacher must be able to see the placement of your body if he is to give an intelligent criticism of your work. Guessing as to what you might be doing under piles of clothing is dangerous! Faulty placement of your body in exercises will weaken and even injure you if you repeat it often enough. You could compare an overdressed dancer to a building that is covered with unnecessary exterior frills that hide its basic structure.

Dance clothing also puts one in the proper frame of mind to work in the dance class. A person usually associates certain activities with a certain kind of clothing. For example, when you swim, you wear a bathing suit. Clothing that restricts movement prevents proper exercising, in the same way that ordinary clothing would restrict the movement of a swimmer when he is in the water. When a dancer has dressed in clothes that he wears only while dancing, he soon associates the clothing with dancing, which, in turn, helps put him in the mood of the experience to come. Conversely, a dancer should not wear dance clothes on the street.

Today's simple dance costume has evolved over many centuries. The first dance costumes were styled after the clothing worn everyday by the dancers in the courts of the sixteenth century. The women wore long, full dresses that hid their bodies and prevented freedom of movement. As time passed and more technical demands were made on the women dancers, their dresses were shortened to permit freer movement. Men's costumes also were simplified until finally a simple leotard was introduced by Jules Léotard, a famous French acrobat, in the mid-nineteenth century. At last dancers could appear without voluminous piles of cloth that restricted and hid movement.

In the ballet, women eventually wore the long "romantic" skirts or the short "classical" skirts that we associate with the "white" ballet today. They also wore toe shoes that allowed them to rise onto the tips of their toes to evoke an ethereal, romantic quality in their movements. The modern dancers broke with this tradition to use simple tights and leotards or free-flowing gowns that allowed more freedom of movement.

Sometimes students or their parents think the wearing of dancer's tights is immoral. Consider the clothing worn on the street today! Tights are modest by comparison.

Most dance schools require special clothing. This clothing can be purchased in most cities or can be ordered by mail when necessary. Check with your teacher before purchasing shoes, tights, or leotards. If the teacher requests shoes, these can be ballet slippers or a modern slipper that sometimes leaves the toes and heels exposed. Most modern dancers do not wear shoes while dancing.

Women's Clothing

Women usually wear tights which cover the legs and hips and a leotard over these which covers the hips and trunk. The seams are worn in the back. Panties or a girdle may be worn under the tights but under no circumstances must these garments be allowed to show beneath the leotard. The showing of the outline of the panty beneath the leotard destroys the long look of the leg. If you feel uncomfortable without panties, perhaps a brief bikini panty will suffice. A well-fitting bra is usually worn.

The tights are usually cut off at the ankle. An elastic band can be sewn on the inside of the tights and pulled down over the instep to pull the wrinkles out of the knees. Some dancers prefer to purchase tights with feet (more expensive), cut the heel and toe out, sew the loose ends to prevent raveling, and wear the remaining arch under the instep.

Dancers seem to delight in finding different ways to wear the dance garments. The only rule to remember is that ordinarily your body must be visually free and clean. Within this rule almost anything goes.

Menstruation is a natural body process which a woman experiences approximately 350 times in her life. If you regard it as a natural phenomenon, it should cause no problems for you. You should take dance class with no hesitation during the menstrual period. If you feel sluggish or slightly uncomfortable, you will probably find you feel much better after the class. Often, stretching can relieve cramps. For the few who have pain associated with the onset of menstruation, what you do is a matter of personal preference. You should not miss more than one class a month. It is too difficult to catch up in the class to indulge yourself the privilege. It must be stressed that if you are contemplating dance as a career, it is not acceptable to miss class. There will be many times when you must audition or perform with cramps or other unpleasant sensations associated with the menstrual period. It is to your advantage to learn to live and to work at such times.

Your teacher understands that you may be embarrassed at having to wear a pad under a tight-fitting leotard. If this bothers you, perhaps an internal tampon would relieve your distress. The tampon is undetectable when in place and does not interfere with movement. It is painless to use and does not disturb the hymen (commonly known as the maidenhead). The use of a tampon is a matter of personal preference. The main consideration is to be comfortable and at ease during the menstrual period. Whatever helps you to enjoy your dance class is acceptable.

Men's Clothing   Men's clothing consists of tights pulled up firmly in the crotch to avoid a baggy, droopy-drawers look. The tights are usually of a heavier material than the women's tights and are designed to fit the male physique. They are less sheer than the women's tights. The seams are worn in the back. A dance belt is worn under the tights to hold the genitals firmly in place and to help prevent ruptures. The one-piece dance belt, about the same size as jockey shorts, gives more support than the athletic supporter (jock-strap) which is ordinarily worn under gym clothes. The dance belt is designed to be worn with the wide cloth part in front. The dance belt is available in either black or white. The belt should be the same color as the tights so that it doesn't show through.

Tights should never hang down in the crotch and distort the body line, a fault that is a clear indication of a beginning student. Male dancers frequently hold the tights up with an ordinary belt around the waist, then roll the tights down over the belt. Others hold the tights up with clip-on suspenders or with elastic bands sewn onto the tights and carried over the shoulders as regular suspenders. The suspenders give a better line in that they eliminate the bulky belt line. A tight-fitting, waist length T-shirt is worn over the torso. This can be tucked into the tights or hang out if it doesn't cover the pelvic area. For both men and women the tights and accessories should be worn so that the silhouette can be seen clearly.

Some dance schools allow dancers to wear gym shorts rather than invest in the special clothing ordinarily worn. The main drawback to shorts is that they do not protect your legs while you are doing floor work, and they do not keep the body heat concentrated in the legs, which helps to keep the muscles warm. They are also not as aesthetically pleasing to the body line as tights.

Tights are made of wool, which is good for cooler climates, and of nylon or a derivative (danskins) which are practical in warmer climates. The wool tights are not as good aesthetically, as they have a tendency to bag and wrinkle at the knees when they become wet with perspiration. Some dancers wear knitted leg-warmers which cover the legs up to the middle of the thigh. These concentrate the heat and help to keep the legs warm.

Tights and leotards are produced in many colors. Some schools insist on uniformity in the colors worn by the students. Check with your teacher before buying colors other than black (worn by both men and women) or pink (customarily reserved for the use of women). If you are allowed to choose your own colors, consider what colors do to the look of your body. If you want to make your body as attractive and slim-appearing as possible, black is for you. The darker colors make you look slimmer. Lighter colors are better on a slim body. If you wear colored tights, it is preferable to wear subdued tones. Remember that bright, garish colors tend to enlarge. The top and the bottom of the outfit should blend harmoniously. A severe contrast in colors tends to visually chop your body into two sections, which is generally not very flattering.

Purchase and Care of Clothing

The initial outlay for dance clothing can be expensive, but it will last for years if properly cared for. Tights and leotards often cost $7 to $10 and a dance belt around $4. Ballet shoes cost approximately $4 to $6, the quality often varying with the price.

Dance clothes should be laundered *after each wearing,* either in warm water alone or with soap and water, in order to prevent fading, rotting, and odor. They should not be stored in a locker when wet with perspiration. Tights sometimes develop runs, which should be sewn as soon as practicable in order to assure a longer life for the garment. In addition, good hygiene and common courtesy indicate a shower after each class.

PERSONAL APPEARANCE

Hair Styles

The hair for both men and women (when the hair styles are long) should be secured in such a way that it does not fall over your face or into your eyes. It is extremely distracting to the dancer and to the audience to

Accessories

have hair that insists on its own creative endeavors. You should find a hair style that is attractive and yet practical for dance.

Before entering the classroom, you should check to see if you have with you all the accessories that might be needed: extra bobby pins, elastic bands for the hair (never for the shoes, as they break and present a physical hazard to everyone working), shoes if required, notebook and pencil if requested. If you perspire heavily, a towel is a good classroom accessory. For those who wear glasses, a strap to hold the glasses securely in place can be purchased at a sporting goods store.

Once the class work has begun, you should be prepared for any clothing emergency that might come up. It is very disturbing to the classroom continuity and to your concentration to be forced to leave the room or stop to adjust clothing. Preparation for such contingencies is the beginning of self-discipline.

Fully prepared, you put on the dance clothes and you walk into the studio to follow in the footsteps of a tradition that spans the centuries. It relates to the basic needs of the primitive tribesman, the courtier of the royal courts, and even to the sophisticated discotheque dancer ecstatically moving to the pounding rhythm of the latest rock music.

CLASS PROCEDURES

As you walk into the studio you are quite likely to see a fairly large room with cylindrical wooden railings (called barres) attached to the walls. The dancer uses these to help his balance while doing exercises. Some studios use a portable metal barre—others do not use barres at all. In the front of the room you might see a large mirror or series of mirrors covering one wall. The floor is usually of hardwood that gives slightly under the weight of the dancer's body, thereby preventing injuries and lessening fatigue. Many professional dancers refuse to dance on concrete. The floor should never be waxed or finished with a lacquer, as most gym floors are. The floor should be washed with water only—never a cleaning agent. Soaps leave a film on the floor which makes the floor slippery. The floor should be free of splinters, nails, and small holes.

Warm-up

As you look around you probably see people dressed in tights, some holding onto the barre, others seated on the floor, all warming up their bodies with simple movements before they begin more strenuous physical activity.

There have been numerous experiments conducted to determine whether or not a warm-up before other exercises has any value. The results of these experiments are contradictory and therefore inconclusive. Some test results state the warm-up was of great value in aiding the performance of athletes, others that there was no significant improvement. Your teacher will have his own theories and methods of working.

As teachers for many years, we have found that the warm-up is valuable for three reasons: such exercise psychologically prepares you to start moving, increases the blood flow, and stimulates sluggish muscles. When a man is frightened, his body shoots adrenalin into the bloodstream, which increases his heartbeat and prepares his body either to fight or to run away. In the classroom an outside stimulus ordinarily is lacking, so simple warm-up exercises may take its place. Let your teacher be your guide.

Simple preparatory exercises could consist of rolling the head in a circle to warm the neck area, circling the shoulders to warm the chest area, slowly stretching upward, sideward, and forward to stretch out the whole body, relaxing the body in a forward slump and then returning to an upright position with tension to activate the reflexes, rolling or flexing the foot at the ankle to warm the ankle, and rising and descending slowly on the ball of the foot to stretch the gastrocnemius (calf muscle).

You should exercise caution about extreme stretching before your body is warmed up. Remember, start slowly and simply.

Accompaniment

Then the teacher walks into the room, possibly accompanied by the pianist who will provide the music for the class. Some teachers use a hand drum to set the rhythm that you will dance to. Perhaps records will provide the accompaniment. The accompaniment will vary according to individual preference of the teacher and more often according to the financial backing of the department or school.

The teacher calls the class from their separate areas of the room, and thus begins your participation in the dance, which the philosopher Havelock Ellis in *The Dance of Life* calls "the source of all the arts that express themselves in the human person." In your new adventure you will explore the natural rhythms and physical movement possibilities of your own body, of nature, and the universe.

Every class has a basic rhythm or form to it. Often the class starts with the warm-up, then moves into the controlled exercises that strengthen your body and develop technique. Usually these exercises are preparing you to do some specific movement exercises for the class on that day. Once you start the class, don't sit down, as your muscles get "cold" and you could needlessly injure yourself. Usually the exercises become more vigorous as the class progresses. Some teachers prefer to end the class with jumps or big movements, others prefer to work the class "down" with tranquil movements so that when you leave you are not as emotionally "high."

Some teachers use the barre in their exercises; others do not. Some teachers do exercises only on the floor or standing; others rarely use the floor. All methods and approaches are valid. All teachers are working toward a similar goal that can be attained in many ways—the goal of developing a beautiful and artistically expressive body for you.

Demonstrations

The teacher will begin the class by demonstrating the movement patterns that he wants you to follow. Unless he specifies that you are to do the movement in your own way, try to copy his way. An important part of dance training is to develop your "artistic eye" to see all the nuances of movement and then reproduce them as demonstrated. There are several reasons: correct execution of exercise is imperative if injuries are to be avoided and physical control is to be established; mastery of the body is part of the satisfaction that comes from dancing; and those who want to be professional dancers must learn movement patterns quickly and correctly. The dance world today is highly competitive and without large financial resources. The choreographer who must produce a work in a limited amount of time, sometimes as little as one week, is forced to hire well-qualified, well-trained dancers who learn quickly and correctly. Dancers who can do any movement required of them by the choreographer are usually hired first. You cannot learn to dance on the job.

Improvisations

Sometimes the teacher, rather than demonstrating a movement pattern, will ask you to improvise movement. If asked to improvise, listen very carefully to the description that he suggests as a basis for the movement. Don't try to intellectualize, plan the movement, or reproduce a movement that you have learned in the classroom. The chief value of improvisation is to free your body with movements that are natural to yourself, to encourage you to be spontaneous, and to stimulate your kinesthetic memory and imagination. Sometimes to stimulate the senses or the imagination, the teacher will ask you to recall a mood, a physical or emotional state of being, movement patterns in space and time, or to imagine how it would feel to be someone or something.

There are many improvisational situations open to the dancer and teacher. (Chapter 6 lists a number of them.) The possibilities are limited only by the limitations of the person who does them. If you can allow yourself to enter into the spirit of the improvisational experience, you will find it very rewarding. It may be the area of movement where you discover whether or not you want to be a dancer, teacher, or choreographer. Improvisation is a very important part of the modern dance experience, equally as important as the mastery of physical technique. Neither should be ignored. One trains the body, the other trains the spirit of the artist-to-be. The synthesis and mastery of the two makes it possible to unite outer discipline and inner joy.

Students usually know how to study in a regular academic class, but are at a loss how to get the most out of a dance class. One of the most important things you can do is to attend every class. Reading a book, this one included, will not teach you how to dance or how to be an artist. You need the daily movement experience to make progress. A crash program in last-minute physical exercises before the final examination will only reward you with fatigue. If your school does not give a final movement examination, then you will probably be graded on your progress in your daily classroom work. If you are given a final movement examination, it will usually deal with the areas of movement that you have had in class and will be evaluated according to how well you understand and execute the movements. Whether you are given an exam or graded in the class, you can only take out of the school what you have gained as a person and as an artist. The pleasure of the experience and self-development should take precedence over grades, even if you are going on to graduate school.

Attendance

When the teacher demonstrates an exercise, watch carefully the flow of the movement and the exact positions the whole body and individual parts of the body take in space. Next, try to move through the exercise by physical

Observing Movement

suggestion of the positions rather than an all-out physical effort. This will develop your kinesthetic sense or motor memory—which are fancy words meaning simply the physical sensation you experience when you watch someone move, as in skating, dancing, falling, or jumping. Next try to do the movement as completely as possible. Watch the other dancers do the movement when you are not working and see if they are doing the same thing the teacher did. Watch the students who move well and ask yourself why they move well and apply it to your own movement. Watch the students who do not move as well and ask yourself why they are not as successful in the exercise. Observing the teacher, other students, and yourself trains your artistic eye to see the design of line, shapes, forms, and movement patterns—all elements of dance. Listen and apply immediately the criticisms your teacher gives you, as well as those given to the class in general. The criticism is offered to help you. It is not an attack on you personally, but rather a criticism to help you master technique. Your teacher is another pair of eyes for you—welcome his comments.

Developing a critical artistic eye is very important to the dancer, but a word of caution is in order. Asserting that you know more than the teacher or other students (even when you do) is undesirable in the classroom unless your opinions are asked for.

Having an open mind to any and all movement is extremely important to the dancer. This presupposes a cooperative spirit with the teacher and others in the classroom. A negative, noncooperative attitude will destroy the efforts of any teacher or fellow artist. A wise teacher—one who knows when to be firm and when to be light in approach—will encourage cooperation and a healthy climate of rapport. He will recognize that intractable discipline and prodding are valid only when they benefit a potential talent. He will welcome intelligent questions and comments. You will gain the most from your classroom experience if you contribute to a spirit of cooperation and helpfulness.

MUSIC

When the teacher demonstrates an exercise, he will usually count out 1 2 3, 1 2 3 4, 1 2 or some other combination of numbers. These individual numbers correspond to certain positions that the body or its parts assume in space or move through in space. When you are asked to repeat the movement, you should attempt to arrive at

these positions on the counts the teacher has indicated.
The counts are then repeated in the music that accompanies the dance sequence you are doing.

Other teachers, instead of giving you specific counts to reach a position on, will give you a phrase of movement that is to correspond to a like musical phrase. A phrase is a certain number of counts or positions that usually make a simple statement. The movement phrase could be likened to a sentence or fragment of a sentence within the spoken language.

A few teachers prefer not to use music, phrases, or counts. They attempt to get you to move so that you sense your own movements in a prescribed or not prescribed time. Whatever method or methods they use, you should know that dance is done in time as well as in space, and you should understand what happens when the same movements are done slow or fast. Develop your musical sense so that you can move to the music or against the music when desired.

In most cases dance is performed to music or some other rhythmical accompaniment, so a basic understanding of common musical forms can be helpful to you. You will be expected to "keep time" with the music. If you study a musical instrument or take a beginning course in musical theory, it will help your dancing by developing your musical appreciation and knowledge. You can help develop your rhythmical sense, which will help you move in time to the beats, by listening to all kinds of music and tapping or clapping out the rhythmical pulse (beat) you feel. As an added exercise, you can try to analyze the structure of the musical piece. You might ask yourself such questions as how the composer has divided up the musical beats you feel, what kind of musical phrases he has used, what moods he has suggested, or what kind of transitions he has used to move from one mood to another mood. Later you might want to study specific musical forms such as the waltz, polka, or mazurka and try to identify these musical forms. If you like the modern sounds of the discotheque dances you might enjoy trying to analyze the structure of these pieces. Try to decide why this music has such a universal appeal. Is it the insistent repetition of a basic beat or the subtle, shifting rhythms? Or is it the words?

There are some basic musical structures that all dancers work with, so you should have some understanding of

Beat

them. When you watch someone unconsciously tapping his foot in time with a piece of music, he usually is tapping the floor in unison with the heavy accents in the music. These are the strong beats that keep the dancers or musicians moving or playing in unison. There are also light beats that precede the repetitious heavy pulses in the music. A light beat occurs when the person you are watching lifts his toes from the floor. A heavy beat occurs when his toes strike the floor.

The light and heavy beats are usually divided into a specific number of counts that are repeated over and over. These repeating series of counts are called bars or measures. For example, two bars would be: and 1 and 2 and 3 and 4; and 1 and 2 and 3 and 4. Each of the bars in this example has four counts. The light beat is indicated by the "and," the heavy beat by the "count." Usually the first "count" of each bar is more heavily accented or sounded than the three following counts.

Measure

In the examples that follow we have listed the most common musical bars that you will probably encounter in your beginning work. (Notice that the "and" counts have been omitted.) The symbol > indicates the strong beat. The ´ indicates the secondary or lighter beat, which means that it is accented more heavily than the other counts but not as heavily as the first count of the bar. The two numbers written as a fraction constitute the musical time signature. The upper number shows how many counts there are in a bar, and the lower number shows what kind of a musical note gets one count. In 2/4 time, for example, there are two counts to a bar and a quarter note gets one. In learning dance, the upper number is more

Rhythm

important. Try clapping the following rhythms, accenting the first count to get their rhythmical feeling.

$\frac{4}{4}$ $\overset{>}{1}$ 2 $\overset{´}{3}$ 4, $\overset{>}{1}$ 2 $\overset{´}{3}$ 4, $\overset{>}{1}$ 2 $\overset{´}{3}$ 4

(three bars of four counts each)

$\frac{3}{4}$ $\overset{>}{1}$ 2 3, $\overset{>}{1}$ 2 3, $\overset{>}{1}$ 2 3

$\frac{2}{4}$ $\overset{>}{1}$ 2, $\overset{>}{1}$ 2, $\overset{>}{1}$ 2

$\frac{6}{8}$ $\overset{>}{1}$ 2 3 $\overset{´}{4}$ 5 6, $\overset{>}{1}$ 2 3 $\overset{´}{4}$ 5 6, $\overset{>}{1}$ 2 3 $\overset{´}{4}$ 5 6

As you have noticed, the 6/8 rhythm has been stressed heavily on the first count and less heavily on the fourth count. Often a 6/8 rhythm is played very quickly by the musician, so is frequently more easily counted by the teacher as $\overset{>}{1}$ 2, $\overset{>}{1}$ 2.

The example shows how the counts would be written in musical notation.

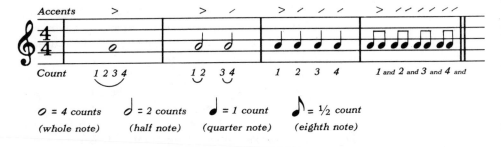

A *triplet* occurs when three notes are played in the time allotted for one note.

The modern dance teacher often experiments with changes in the rhythmical form. He may change the number of counts in the basic musical bars to give variety. You might be asked to dance to a series of bars like 1̌ 2 3, 1̌ 2 3 4, or 1̌ 2, 1̌ 2 3 or some other combination of rhythms. This is referred to as *mixed meter*.

Another musical change you might encounter in the dance class is called *shifted accent*. Instead of accenting the first count, as you might expect, the accent falls on another count. For example:

1̌ 2 3, 1 2̌ 3, 1 2̌ 3, 1 2 3̌
1 2 3̌, 1 2̌ 3, 1̌ 2 3, 1̌ 2 3

In this example the expected heavy accent in the third, fourth, fifth, and sixth bars has been shifted to a count other than the first count, resulting in a feeling of syncopation. *Syncopation* can be shifting the accent, but is more often beginning a note on an unaccented beat and continuing the note without a new accent into the ordinarily accented beat. For example: clap the "ands" and "counts" of the following rhythm—*don't* clap the following count when it is tied together with a bow:
1 2 3 and⌢1 2 3 and⌢1 2 3 and⌢1 2 3.
The silence on the count of one makes the syncopation.

Cumulative rhythm occurs when each new bar has one more count added to it. For example: 1̌, 1̌ 2, 1̌ 2 3, 1̌ 2 3 4.

Diminution of rhythm is the exact opposite of cumulative rhythm. Each new bar has one count subtracted from it. For example: 1̌ 2 3 4, 1̌ 2 3, 1̌ 2, 1̌.

Tempo refers to the speed of the musical accompaniment or dance movement. *Changes in tempo* from very slow to very fast or the reverse result in a change of the quality of the movement. If your teacher changes the tempo of the movement, observe its effect on the movement. Changes in tempo sometimes make otherwise dreary movement quite exciting to watch.

Dancers do not always dance with the reoccurring beat of the music. This would soon lead to boredom. To add interest the dancers also move on the "offbeat" or against the prevailing rhythm. If you clap the counts below with the accents indicated above them, you will feel the sense of *double time,* or doubling of the basic beat. Each of the bars should take exactly the same amount of time to clap.

1 2 3 4, 1 and 2 and 3 and 4 and, 1 2 3 4, 1 and 2 and 3 and 4 and

The second and fourth bars are rhythmically doubled in counts but not in time. A colloquial form of the "double time" often used in jazz dancing is: 1 and 2 3 and 4, 1 and 2 3 and 4.

A colloquial "single rhythm" is:

1 and 2 3 4, 1 and 2 3 4, or 1 2 3 and 4, 1 2 3 and 4. In the first and second bars, the single rhythm occurs on 1 and 2. In the third and fourth bars the single rhythm occurs on 3 and 4.

Part of the pleasure of the classroom experience will be the thrill of exploring with your teacher the various rhythmical possibilities, and also the qualities and forms of movement described in the next chapter. When the teacher has demonstrated and led you through a movement combination, he will no doubt say something like "ready and one." The "ready" is your warning to ready yourself to move. The "and" tells you to set your body in motion to move into your first position on the count of "one."

Translating the rhythms and moods of the music into movements in space and time leads you toward the discipline that you must acquire if you are to eventually express to an audience your pleasure in moving. The same discipline will permit you to express your thoughts and feelings in dance. If you choose dance as a career, the discipline will help you contribute to your art as a dancer, choreographer, or teacher.

"What we do not understand, we do not possess."
—Goethe

Technique Analysis

The development of modern dance as an art form came about by breaking the "rules" of what dance was "supposed" to be. The traditions and techniques of modern dance continue to evolve as new gifted artists change the rules. Such change is a healthy thing. An art form can only grow when new ideas and new modes of expression come into it.

One of the exciting elements of the modern dance is the distorted use of lines, shapes, and forms to achieve a new aesthetic of beauty. Any line, any shape, any form that the human body can possibly assume in space is valid to the modern dancer if it expresses what the dancer wants to communicate. Some of you in the beginning may think the movements you are asked to do are "ugly." If you should feel that way, think of the movements as a challenge to see if you can find any similar shapes and forms in the world around you, and then try to understand their validity in an art form.

You should be aware of a few basic points about natural body alignment in order to better understand the deviations from it. Think of your natural alignment as "good posture." Think of your body being stretched upward from your foot support through the top of your head. The stretch is as if you were holding onto a bar over your head and hanging down from it. Think of a straight line running down from the top of your head through your neck, torso, pelvis, and legs. This line is the central axis of your body. When you are standing, jumping, kneeling, or sitting in a good posture, be aware that your head,

DEVELOPMENT IN TECHNIQUE

Basic Alignment

19

chest, and pelvic area stay in a straight vertical line. Your shoulders should be comfortably pulled down and back.

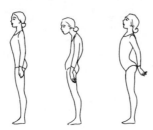

People with bad posture may slump forward so that their shoulders are rounded, or release their pelvis backward, causing a sway-back. Avoid both distortions of line.

The following illustrations provide a few ideas for you to consider in your basic alignment.

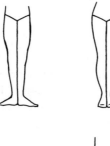

You should hold good alignment through various degrees of *leg rotation*. The legs can be turned out from the hip socket or held so that the feet are pointed forward in a parallel position.

You should have *weight placement on the feet* evenly divided in a tripod between the big toe, the little toe, and the heel. When you rise to the ball of the foot (to half-toe), your weight should be between the big toe and the second toe, never toward the little toe.

Good alignment of the leg is essential to support in a *knee bend*. You should keep the center of the knee in line with the middle toe. In the small knee bend (demi-plié), the heels usually remain on the floor. In the deep knee bend (grand plié) the heels usually leave the floor naturally, in order to prevent a pushing backward in the pelvis with a subsequent lean forward in the torso.

To *balance on one leg,* you should pull up on the vertical line through the body. Don't "sit" into the supporting leg. Shift the hip toward the supporting leg and on a slight diagonal upward. In the basic balance on one leg, keep the two front pelvic bones straight across on a horizontal line.

Most modern dancers have not codified the terms for the positions and movements as thoroughly as the ballet dancers have done. A number of modern dancers feel that codification of terms would inhibit free expression and would prevent new forms of technique from developing. Another reason against codification is the infinite variety of positions the body can assume in space: any code of modern dance movement would have to be limited and arbitrary. We have attempted to give names to body positions *only as a guide* to analyzing the infinite movement possibilities of the body. The names should be thought of as a springboard to further exploration and body analysis and not as an attempt at definitive codification.

Your teacher will use his own terms. Whatever they are, it is valuable for you to learn them so that when he refers to something like "axial movement" (movement around the axis of your body) you will immediately associate this with the kind of movement or position he wants. For the purposes of analysis, definitions of basic positions are desirable. Then you as a student can identify each basic position and can understand the further development of that position. This helps you learn faster and helps to train the "artistic eye" to see the subtleties of movement.

FIRST ANALYSIS   *Movements in a Stationary Position*

While in a stationary position, you have only a few basic possibilities of movement: you may bend, rotate, push, or support yourself in various ways. Despite the limited number of basic movements, many variations are possible, and a stationary position presents opportunities as well as restrictions. The drawings on the next page show a few of the variations.

Bend The *whole leg* can bend from the hip socket and move in any direction, to a certain level, with or without rotation in the hip socket and with or without a bend in the lower leg. The *foot* can stretch forward to a "pointed" foot position or bend back to a "flexed" foot position with or without rotation. The *arm* and *hand* have more freedom of movement, but are similar to the leg and foot in bending with or without rotation. The *torso* can bend in any direction with a rounded back or straight back, to a specific level, with or without body rotation. The bend can be in the chest area (more limited bending) or from the hips (greater bending). The *head* can bend in some direction independently from whatever position the torso is in.

Rotate The *head, shoulders, torso,* and *hips* can all rotate around their own axes separately or together. The hips can rotate under and back as well as in a sideward rotation. The whole body can revolve completely around on its own axis (turn).

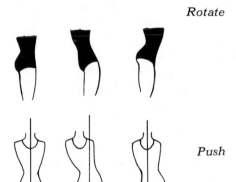

Push The *head, shoulders, ribcage,* and *hips* can push as a unit from their central axis in some direction.

Support The *body* can be supported on the floor by sitting, kneeling, or standing. It can leave the floor by jumping or being lifted and held.

As a means of movement and position analysis you could ask yourself various questions. Concerning bending, you could inquire: What part of the body is bending and to what level? Is the bend curved or sharply angled?

About rotation, you could ask: What part or parts are rotated and in what direction? If the whole body is turning, which hip is pulled back? Is it a complete turn or only a fraction of a turn? Is the turn on one foot or both feet? What is the position of the body in the turn?

As for pushing, you could raise two questions: What part of the body is being pushed and in what direction? Is the push only a basic impulse to move into another position? And about support, you could ask: What are the positions leading to a certain level of support?

Dance is, of course, more than just stationary positions. Dance is moving the whole body through space from one position to another. The motivation behind the movement will change the look and feel of the movement.

SECOND ANALYSIS   Body Lines

Three basic lines can be achieved in dance. These lines may be formed by parts of the body or by the dancer's entire body as shown in the illustrations:

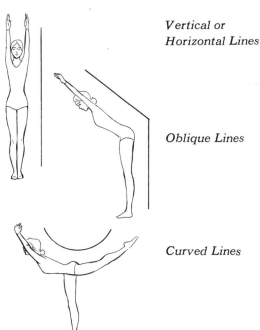

Vertical or horizontal lines occur when the dancer stands upright or bends at a right angle or lies on the floor. Such lines also may be achieved in many other ways.

Vertical or Horizontal Lines

Oblique (slanted) lines occur when the dancer bends at an obtuse or an acute angle in relation to either a horizontal or a vertical. Oblique lines may be formed in many ways.

Oblique Lines

Curved lines occur in various positions. These lines, like the others, may be combined with the others, just as oblique lines may be combined with horizontals or verticals or both.

Curved Lines

As line is so important in the dance, you should *visually trace* the line of movement your teacher demonstrates and try to approximate the line he shows. Sometimes you may think another line looks better or feels better for you, but remember that part of the self-discipline of learning the dance craft is to make your body do anything that choreography requires.

THIRD ANALYSIS   *Feet, Body, and Arm Positions*

Feet Positions

Many modern dancers use some modified version of the five ballet feet positions. The ballet dancer arrives at the feet positions by turning out the legs at the hip sockets until, in the ideal turn-out, the toes are pointing directly to the sides of the body. The five *ballet* feet positions follow:

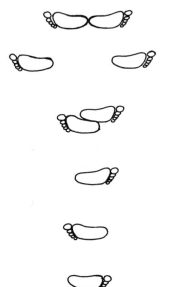

In the *first* position, the heels are together.

In the *second* position, the heels are about twelve inches apart.

The front heel is next to the instep of the back foot and the feet are touching in the *third* position. *This position is seldom used.*

In the *fourth* position, one foot is about twelve inches in front of the other.

The front heel is next to the toe of the back foot and the feet are touching in the *fifth* position.

Here are three modifications of the first position:

The *diagonal* modification requires turn-out in the hip sockets so that the toes point on diagonal lines.

In the *parallel* version, the legs are not turned out or in and the toes point forward.

In the *diagonal-in* modification, the legs are turned in from the hip sockets so that the toes point on diagonal lines inward (this position is occasionally used in modern dance).

For purposes of analysis, the following definitions hold. The definitions use the basic foot positions as reference points. As the illustrations show, the definitions include various body lines as well as movements in a stationary position.

Body Positions

In the *first* position, the feet and legs are together.

Standing   Sitting   Bending

In the *second* position, the feet and legs are apart to the side.

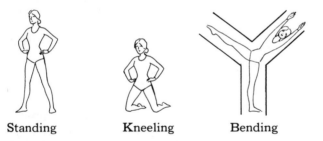

Standing   Kneeling   Bending

In the *fourth* position, the feet and legs are apart, one foot to the front and the other to the back.

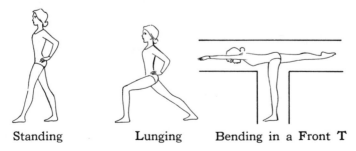

Standing   Lunging   Bending in a Front T

In the *third* or *fifth* position, the legs and feet cross one another in some manner (the third and the fifth positions are combined here because the placement of feet is so similar).

Standing   Jumping   Curving in a Side Arc

Arm Positions

In the analysis of arm positions we again turn to basic ballet as a reference. Because the arm is more flexible than other parts of the body, more movement possibilities exist. Not all ballet schools will agree with the analysis below. Other basic arm positions may be defined, but the descriptions and illustrations here are a useful guide.

In the *first* position, the arms are down at the sides of the body.

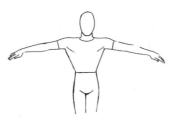

In the *second* position, the arms are raised to the sides of the body in a horizontal plane.

One arm is raised to the side and the other arm is to the front—high or middle or low —in the *third* position.

The arms are in front of the body but not on the same level in the *fourth* position.

In the *fifth* position, the arms are in front of the body and are on the same level.

Examples of some variations of these arm positions follow. (With bending in the torso or rotations in the shoulder sockets, the positions also can be approximated behind the back.)

First   Second   Third

Fourth   Fifth

You might want to experiment, using the basic positions as a guide, to see how many variations you can discover by rotating the arms in the sockets, by changing the directions and levels of the arms, and by changing the degree of bend in the elbows.

In watching classroom demonstrations, ask the same sorts of questions that were applied to the analysis of movements in a stationary position: Are the arms straight or bent? In what direction? What is the angle of bend? Are the arms rotated inward or outward or are they "normal"? Is the basic line curved or angular?

FOURTH ANALYSIS   *Movement*

Dance is, of course, more than static positions in space. Some schools simplify the analysis of movement into two categories: *nonlocomotor movement,* which means movement around your own axis, above a stationary support, and *locomotor movement,* which means movement through space to get yourself from one place to another.

In our analysis of basic movements in a stationary position—bending, rotating, pushing, and going to various support positions—we described nonlocomotor movements. However, these movements also can be done while moving from one place to another. Similarly, many of the movements described below can be done *either* while traveling in space or while remaining in one place.

There are six kinds of movement in the analysis here. How they are done (quality or dynamics) and why they are done (motivation) provide infinite variations.

Descending or Rising Movement

Your body can descend toward the floor, as in a deep knee bend, or rise away from the floor, as in a jump. The individual parts of your body can also move toward or away from the floor.

Outward Movement

An outward movement is any kind of movement that goes away from your body, as a leg kick to the front.

Inward Movement

An inward movement is any kind of movement that comes toward the center of your body, as when you pull your outstretched arms toward your chest.

Turns

There are three kinds of turns: (1) You can twist or rotate *part of your body* on its central axis. (2) You can turn *your whole body* around in a circle. There are many ways such turns can be done; for example, on your own axis on two feet, on one foot, from one foot to the other foot, or while jumping. (3) You can turn in *a traveling pattern;* for example, by walking in a circle around a chair or by doing a series of turns while traveling in a straight line.

Falls

There are two basic kinds of falls. In one you fall off-balance but catch yourself before you go to the floor. In

the second you fall and allow yourself to go all the way
to the floor. Both are controlled but usually have the sense
of going with the pull of gravity. A recovery is the action
that follows the fall.

Movement of the entire body in some direction through *Traveling*
space is traveling. There are many ways of traveling and
they employ the other movement patterns. The eight
traveling (locomotor) movements that have become standard in modern dance follow (some of them you can also
do in place, rather than traveling): (1) *Walk*. (2) *Run*.
(3) *Hop* by jumping off one foot or two feet and landing
on one foot. (4) *Skip* by doing a step and a hop, alternating from one foot to the other. (5) *Slide* by moving the
front foot forward, transferring the weight to the front
foot; then slide the back foot toward the front foot, placing
the weight onto the back foot with a "cutting" action, which
forces the front foot to lift quickly. (6) *Gallop* (similar to
the slide, only done in the air) by doing a step and a hop
off the forward leg. While in the air pull the back leg to
the front leg in a cutting motion and land on the back leg,
at the same time lifting the front leg quickly. The front
foot always maintains a forward lead. (7) *Leap* by doing
a large jump from one foot to the other foot. The body
traces an arc in space. (8) *Jump* by going from one foot
or two feet, landing on both feet.

Some variations of traveling movements are: (1) *Prance* *Variations of*
by alternating the feet with a sharp emphasis on the bent, *Traveling*
forward-lifted free leg, like a trotting horse. (2) A *triplet*
is made up of three steps. Bend on the first step, rise to
the half-toe with straight legs on the next two steps, and
repeat smoothly any number of times with the first bending step being alternately on one foot, then the other foot.
(3) In a *dart,* the emphasis of the movement is outward
on the horizontal plane, rather than jumping upward. Step
repeatedly on the same foot and then jump onto the free
foot, or jump repeatedly from one foot to the other. (4)
Glide by smoothly moving across the floor in some pattern.

FIFTH ANALYSIS   *Qualities or Dynamics*

All movement patterns take on a different look when
you change their qualities or dynamics. If a pattern fails
to convey some quality it becomes devoid of any human
association, and it will have little appeal to a general
audience.

We have chosen to consider qualities as related to the science of *dynamics*. Dynamics concerns the motion of bodies and their motivating forces. It is related to the greater or lesser use of energy by your body while moving in time or space. The movement is motivated by the need to express some kind of emotional or physical state. There are a number of basic qualities that can add "shading" to your movement in the same way a painter uses contrasts in colors and shapes to enrich his painting.

The inner motivation for the movement is elusive, but the external movement can be analyzed. For purposes of analysis we have divided the qualities or dynamics into four basic areas: speed of movement, contrasting energy forces, combined energy forces, and spatial emphasis.

Speed of Movement

In terms of speed, a movement may change or remain the same: (1) A movement that remains the same may be *fast* or *slow* or *in between*. (2) Change occurs when the movement *accelerates* or *retards*. The musical terms "accelerando" and "ritardando" are sometimes applied to these changes in dance movement.

Contrasting Energy Forces

There are four main kinds of contrasting energy forces: (1) An effort to move some object may be a *push* or a *pull*. The effort may work against a real object, such as a very heavy rock, or against an imaginary force. (2) A movement may be *light* or *heavy*. A light movement will convey a feeling of effortlessness and ease, as when you swim underwater. A heavy movement will seem labored, as when you carry a heavy object. (3) *Relaxation* and *tension* are contrasting qualities of energy forces. A movement may have the relaxed feeling that your body has when you let it go limp, or it may have the tense feeling that occurs when you clench your hand tightly into a fist. (4) A movement may be *sharp* or *fluid*. A sharp movement is percussive, as when you knock loudly on a door, and a fluid movement is smooth and flowing, as when you glide across the ice on skates.

Combined Energy Forces

There are several combined movement dynamics commonly used in modern dance: (1) A relaxed *sway* is similar to the swaying motion of tree branches in the wind. The sway also can be done with tension in the body, which will give a different feel and look to the movement. The sway implies more flexibility and less regularity than the swing. (2) The *swing* and the sway both imply a movement back and forth or up and down. The swing usually is suspended momentarily before it retraces its path, like the pendulum of a clock. The swing often is regular, but it may be irregular instead. (3) *Suspension* means a temporary stopping of movement. It is like the brief moment on a roller coaster ride when the car reaches the crest before plunging down the slope. Similar movement is frequently used in dance to achieve, at least subliminally, such a sensation of suspense. (4) A *fall* usually has the same feeling of suspension that the swing has, only the pull of gravity takes over and the body sinks toward the floor with an increase in speed. The fall conveys the feeling of going toward the floor with the pull of gravity. An *off-balance* fall, in contrast, conveys the sense of losing balance briefly but regaining control of the fall before it completes the downward cycle. (5) The *shake* is a vibratory motion that is similar to the shaking you experience when you are very cold. The dance of the Charleston frequently employs the hands in a rapid pivoting motion at the wrist, a typical shaking motion.

All of these combined quality movements can be done with the whole body or a part of the body.

Spatial emphasis occurs in the following movement dynamics: (1) A *crescendo* is exhibited by a movement that starts small and then increases its use of space. Quite often a crescendo is done in a swinging movement. (2) A *decrescendo* starts large and becomes smaller. (3) *Accents* in terms of space come about when the main emphasis of a movement is up, down, out, or in. (4) An *outward focus* is provided by a movement that goes away from your body (as described in the analysis of basic movement, both locomotor and nonlocomotor). An outward emphasis occurs when the movement's motivation is directed to the outside. (5) An *inward focus* occurs when the movement's motivation is directed internally. (6) The *path of movement* can be a straight line, a curved line, or a combination of both, and the emotional intent or quality of a movement can be changed according to the path taken. For example, a very self-assured man might extend his hand forward in a straight, direct line toward his partner. A grandiose lady might extend her hand toward her suitor in a curved, florid gesture. A shy person might extend, withdraw, extend, and finally make contact.

Spatial Emphasis

SIXTH ANALYSIS *Floor Patterns*

Basically, floor patterns are made up of curves, straight lines, or combinations of both. The patterns are more intricate than the paths of movement described above. A few of the basic patterns are shown below. As a means of movement exploration, try applying these basic floor patterns to movement patterns or to stationary positions of the body. (They all can be done with the whole body or parts of the body.) The arrow indicates the direction of travel and the square represents the performance area.

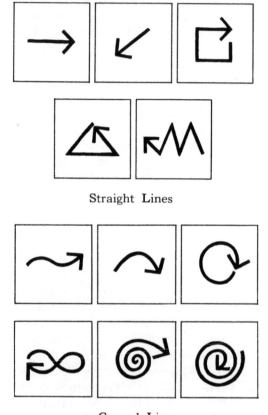

Straight Lines

Curved Lines

These six sets of analyses are offered to help you learn to dance more quickly by using your mind as well as your body. Your teacher will stress some of these ideas and reject others. All approaches are valid if they help you reach your goal as a dancer.

"...frequently the most talented people are those most aware of their own deficiencies and most willing to work hard to overcome them."

—Lee Strasberg

CHAPTER 4

Anatomy, Injuries, Diet

It is to your advantage to be familiar with the terms your teacher uses when referring to anatomy. There are definite correct and incorrect ways to work your body to receive the maximum results from your effort. If you know in advance what part of the body your teacher is talking about, you can immediately apply your anatomical knowledge to the correct execution of the exercise.

BASIC ANATOMY

We are presenting to you only the basic anatomical facts and physiological principles from which to work. If you are interested in a more thorough study, we have listed some excellent references in the selected readings.

In a single dance exercise almost every muscle in the body is used. In the charts that follow we have indicated only the large, main groups of movers and their common functions and movements. You can dance without knowing about these muscles, but a brief introduction to them should help you to understand dance movement better.

A vigorous dance class after a period of inactivity may cause muscle soreness, the most common pain resulting from dance classes. Although it is uncomfortable, the pain is temporary and is not debilitating. At the moment when you are sore you may feel as if you could not take another step, let alone take a dance class. There are many theories why the muscles become so sore. Regardless of the reason, the best way to relieve your pain is to work the muscle again, and as soon as possible. A hot bath or shower and a

INJURIES, ETC.
Muscle Soreness

33

PART OF BODY	MAIN MUSCLES	APPROXIMATE LOCATION	MAIN MOVEMENT
ARMS AND SHOULDER	TRICEPS	Bottom of upper arm (when arm is lifted to side at right angle to body with palm up)	Straightens or extends bow
	BICEPS	Top of upper arm (when arm is lifted to side at right angle to body with palm up)	Bends or flexes elbow
	PECTORALS	Front of chest	Rotate arm inward shoulder socket and co trol some other a movements
	TRAPEZIUS AND OTHER MUSCLES OF THE UPPER BACK	Upper back	Move scapulae (shoul blades)
ABDOMEN	OBLIQUUS	Over ribs on either side	Twists upper body either side
	RECTUS ABDOMINIS	From upper ribs to top of pubic bone, covering abdomen area	Raises upper body f ward as in sit-up
	QUADRATUS LUMBORUM	Small of back	1. Bends upper body side 2. Stabilizes pelvis a spine
HIP AND UPPER LEG (THIGH)	GLUTEALS	Buttocks	1. Stabilize hip 2. Extend hip
	QUADRICEPS	Front of thigh	Extends leg in forwa movements
	HAMSTRINGS	Back of upper leg	Bend knee
LOWER LEG	GASTROC-NEMIUS (GASTROX OR CALF)	Back of lower leg	1. Points foot 2. *Raises* leg to ball foot (half-toe) 3. Bends knee
	SOLEUS	Back of lower leg under gastrox muscle	*Holds* leg in half-toe sition (ball of foot)
	TIBIALIS AND PERONEUS	Around either side of ankle	Move ankle in circle
	ACHILLES TENDON	Lower part of leg and heel on back of leg; lower part of gastrox (calf) muscle	Same as gastrox

COMMON EXERCISE TO STRENGTHEN OR USE	SIGNIFICANCE TO DANCE	COMMON INJURY AND PREVENTION
sh up	1. Needed by male for lifts 2. Gives firmness under the arm 3. Strengthens arms	None
sh up and pull up	1. Needed by male for lifts 2. Strengthens arms	None
sh up	1. Provide firm chest muscles 2. Needed by male for lifts	None
sh up	Give control of back and arms	None
ist or rotate upper body	Makes small, strong waist	None
up	Keeps abdomen flat if used constantly	None
Bend upper body to side Sit up	Contributes to strong lower back	*Injury*—General weakness *Prevention*—Use
Turn out the leg from hip socket Walk (especially rapid) Run	Permit thigh turn-out	None
Lift leg forward Straighten leg at knee joint Pull up knee cap	1. Steadies knee joint 2. Straightens knee	*Injury*—Charley-horse *Prevention*—At onset of pain, rest until pain stops
Touch toes with fingers without bending knees Sit erect on floor with legs extended straight forward Bend knees	1. Bend knee 2. Must be stretched constantly	*Injury*—Cramps *Preveniton*—At onset of pain, rest until pain stops
ump Rise to ball of foot	1. Tires easily 2. Main muscle in jump	*Injury*—Temporary soreness from sudden overuse *Prevention*—Should be used constantly
e to ball of foot and *hold*	1. Points foot 2. *Holds* leg in half-toe position	None
ate ankle in circle	1. Help protect Achilles tendon 2. Support ankle in all foot movements	*Injury*—Sprained ankle *Prevention*—Keep ankle in line with center of knee
ıp	1. Must be stretched constantly 2. Thickest and strongest tendon in body	*Injury*—Tears apart by violent overstretching *Prevention*—When coming down from a jump, land on ball of foot, lower heel to floor, bend leg

massage feel marvelous, but actually do little more than relax you and make you feel better temporarily.

Pain from Injuries   Pain resulting from an injury is an entirely different feeling, and proper care of the injured part must be administered to prevent possible permanent damage. For the most part, an injury occurs when a part of your body is weak and/or when you are tired physically or psychologically or both. In any class, if you are in good physical condition and if you work correctly, injuries should rarely occur. However, a few common physical problems are discussed here. It is assumed that if you have severe, recurring pain, you will see your doctor, and if you have any injury, you will report it to your teacher.

Cramp   A common pain is the cramp. A cramp is an overfatigue of a muscle and is probably caused from a lack of calcium and salt in the diet. It usually occurs in the arch of the foot or the calf of the leg. The pain occurs because the muscle goes into a maximum contraction involuntarily. To relieve a cramp, try to stretch the cramped part very gently or massage it in order to get a fresh blood supply to it. Generally, no permanent damage results from a cramp, but the muscle may be sore. Usually you may continue dancing as soon as severe pain subsides.

Sprain   A much more serious injury is the sprain. This injury occurs to a joint when a bone goes past its normal range of movement and tissue is torn. This does not heal easily and demands a doctor's care. Ligaments and capsules in the hip and shoulder may be injured in this manner, but more commonly the injury takes place in the ligaments of the ankle. Generally, something wet and cold should be applied to the area until a doctor can be consulted. He should be called or the injured dancer taken to him immediately. To prevent a sprained ankle it is extremely important that the ankle be centered with the knee at all times, especially when landing from a jump or leap. To prevent a sprain in the hip, you must never turn out beyond your range. If you are prone to a sprain in any part of your body, consult your doctor or teacher for exercises to strengthen that part.

Strain   A strain is caused when a muscle is overtired from constant irritation by overcontraction of muscles. It affects muscle tendons and soft tissue. This pain can be relieved by rest. It usually happens in the gastrox (calf muscle) and hamstrings (back of thigh). Strains rarely result from taking just one class.

The charley-horse is an injury which usually occurs in the quadriceps (front of thigh) and can be remedied by standing on the leg and massaging it gently.

A more serious injury is the shin splint. This occurs only to the muscles on the front of the tibia (shin bone). Shin splints are believed to be the tearing of the muscle from the bone which may cause severe pain. An improper landing from a jump with the heels off the floor and with no bend in the knee seems to cause shin splints. A doctor should always be consulted when shin splints or any other injury occurs.

Other kinds of injuries could occur in a dance class, but they are few and very uncommon. It cannot be stressed enough that if you work properly, injuries should not occur.

Modern dance should not produce the bulky muscles familiar to a football player or to a wrestler. These sport activities warrant the development of heavy muscles for strength. As a dancer you need long, lean lines so that the clarity of the movement is not clouded. You need minimum weight so that you can perform intricate movements easily.

You as a dancer must convey the ideal physique or figure. No one has a perfect body! But by proper dance training and a proper balance of exercise, rest, and diet, you can more quickly achieve the illusion of the ideal.

Dancers are notoriously abusive of their bodies. They often expect their bodies to respond instantly and perfectly on command without having given them proper care. You cannot expect to deal with the great physical demands made on your body without intelligently caring for it.

The word "diet" often suggests hunger, regimented eating, or eating only certain kinds of food for extended periods. To the dancer, diet should signify temperance in living habits. It simply means that the dancer must make an intelligent consideration of the consequences of his living habits.

As a dancer, you cannot afford extra calories in foods which do not make an appreciable contribution to your body. Even if you are of a good weight, size, and structure to be a dancer, it is to your advantage to evaluate your daily intake of food.

Your body needs specific foods every day. You need at least two portions of a high protein food such as meat, poultry, fish, eggs, peas or beans. You need one or more servings of green or yellow vegetables, and one or more servings of fruits (including citrus fruits). In addition, you should have two servings of a cereal product (this includes bread). You should have milk or milk products daily.

You need a normal amount of salt and other vitamins and minerals daily. In some cases of overweight, it is suggested that salt be eliminated from the diet. Salt should not be eliminated from the dancer's diet as the dancer sweats a great deal and loss of salt through perspiration can cause extreme exhaustion and even prostration during class. (It also is extremely important that a dancer drink from four to six glasses of water a day to offset loss of water through perspiration.) You should continue your normal intake of salt and not worry about it except during excessive heat or prolonged exercise.

*Fad Diets and
Other Temptations*

Certain fad diets seem to be the folly of the dancer. The dancer exists on grapefruit, tomatoes and cottage cheese, vegetables, or low-calorie beverages for a week or so. Then, to ease the hunger pains, he devours one large pizza, two banana splits, and three enchiladas plus various side dishes of french fries, potato chips, cookies, and doughnuts. Within one hour, his whole week's regimen is destroyed. To lose weight and keep it lost, he must control his way of eating. This is the "magic elixir" leading to maximum energy and a beautiful body.

Because you are dancing and must keep your strength level high, be sure that you do not eliminate proteins, vegetables, fruits, milk products, and whole grain cereals from your diet. It is important and relatively easy to eliminate fried foods, pastries, and carbonated beverages. It is more difficult but not impossible to eliminate eating at drive-ins, ice cream parlors, and delicatessens. The latter produce delicious, appealing foods, but if you are watching your food intake, you simply cannot indulge your taste buds at these places.

*Evaluating
Your Diet*

The following is a suggested way to evaluate your eating habits. First, keep an *exact* record of the amount of everything you eat for three days. Do not change the way you usually eat. Buy a small calorie counter (you can get one at any drug or grocery store for less than a dollar) and count the number of calories you have consumed in these three days. Divide by three and you will find the average amount you eat daily. To lose one pound a week permanently, you have to cut 500 calories a day from your diet, provided you have not increased your activity level.

If you increase the amount you exercise, you can lose weight at a faster rate. Often, though, exercise increases your appetite and weight is gained, not lost. Exercise may tone your muscles and you may find your measurements are smaller, but you have not lost weight. You must find a point of balance between exercise and food intake. As a rough guide, 3,500 calories make up one pound of fat.

A female dancer can usually determine the amount of calories her body needs to _maintain_ the desired weight by multiplying it by eleven or twelve, depending upon her metabolic rate (the rate she burns up food). This means if her desired weight is 100 pounds, she can probably maintain it by eating 1,100 to 1,200 calories a day. A male should be able to multiply his weight by twelve or thirteen or perhaps more to maintain his desired weight.

You will have to experiment to find your food intake level. Remember, you need approximately 60 grams of protein a day to supply the body's needs. Your individual needs will depend on how much you exercise and whether or not you have reached maturity.

Day-to-Day Dieting

When you have determined how much you _can_ eat, you have to carefully choose _what_ you eat, for within this calorie limitation you must include the necessary foodstuffs, as previously listed. To start your diet, weigh yourself after your largest meal, preferably in the evening. Weigh yourself with the same amount of clothing on every time. After your initial weighing, _never_ again weigh yourself in the evening. Now start your diet the next morning. Weigh yourself the _following_ morning. You will find that you weigh two or three pounds less than you did from your last weighing. You haven't really lost weight, but it gives you a good feeling to start off your diet with. From that point on, only weigh yourself every two or three days. You will find you reach plateaus and hold a weight for a time. Don't be discouraged, stay on your diet. Of course, it is assumed that you _consult your doctor before starting any diet_ to make sure your overweight or underweight condition is not due to an illness.

Diet pills are not a desirable method by which to lose weight. They may take away your normal appetite but they do not change dietary habits. It is often found that users of so-called diet pills gain back the lost weight as soon as they quit taking the pills. It is of great importance for you not to be dependent on an artificial means to find and maintain your dancer's body.

We do not go into the problem of the underweight person. A dancer, it seems, cannot be too slim. It is important, though, that with the extreme slimness of the dancer there is also a high degree of physical strength. If you are slim but weak, we suggest you see your doctor for a check-up. As far as dance is concerned, slimness on the female body, even going so far as being "skinny" (as defined by parents), is an asset. The male dancer's physique should be well-muscled without excess fat or bulk.

Here, in brief, are some important guides to dieting: (1) Try not to eat between meals. If you must eat, try raw carrots, celery, turnips, radishes, or cauliflower. Drink water. (2) Eat at least three normal meals a day or five smaller meals. (Make sure they are small.) (3) Eat fresh fruit and low-calorie gelatine, sherbet, or custard for dessert. (4) If you must splurge on a high calorie food item, then you must make up for it the next day by lowering the caloric intake. (5) Coffee and tea have zero calories provided they have no sugar and cream added to them. (6) Drink four to six glasses of water a day. You will be burning fat and a large intake of water helps elimination.

CALORIE CONTENT OF VARIOUS FOODS

Food	Amount	Calories	Grams of Protein
Apple pie	1/7 section	331	3
Asparagus	4 oz.	20	3
Brownie	2" x 2" x ¾"	135	4
Cola carbonated beverage	12 oz.	156	3
Cottage cheese	½ cup (4 oz.)	90	19
Halibut, broiled	4 oz.	205	29
French fries	8 pieces, 2" x ½" x ½"	157	2
Hamburger with lettuce and tomato	1 average, 3½" diameter	650	30
Lettuce and tomato salad	4 oz.	30	2
Pizza	1 section of small pizza, 9" diameter	245	14
Potato chips	1 large, 3" diameter	15	0
Sugar doughnut with hole	1 doughnut	200	3
Vanilla ice cream	1 scoop (4 oz.)	150	3
Yogurt, plain	½ cup	60	4

"For last year's words belong to last year's language
And next year's words await another voice."
—T. S. Eliot

CHAPTER 5

History

The dance discussed in this book has been developed in the last eighty years. It was called "modern" because it broke from the traditions and the disciplines of the stiff formality of the ballet of the last century. At the beginning, modern dance was a way of life, an expression of the freedom of spirit, unfettered by outdated traditions and worn-out beliefs. Modern dance was in its adolescence at the time of the movement for women's suffrage, Prohibition, World War I, and new movements in art. One such movement was called expressionism. Expressionism originated in painting. It is a subjective expression of the artist's personal reactions to events or objects through distortion, abstraction, or symbols. It was a dominating influence on the modern dance.

PIONEERS IN DANCE

Many artists late in the last century were in search of a means to express their individuality and concern for man. Modern dance was one of the ways some of these people sought to free their creative spirit. At the beginning there was no exacting technique, no foundation from which to build. In later years trial, error, and genius founded the techniques and the principles of the movement. Eventually, innovators even drew from what they considered the dread ballet, but first they had to discard all that was academic so that the new could be discovered. The beginnings of modern dance were happening before Isadora Duncan, but she was the first person to bring the new dance to general audiences and see it accepted and acclaimed.

Isadora Duncan

Her search for a natural movement form sent her to

41

nature. She believed movement should be as natural as the swaying of the trees and the rolling waves of the sea, and should be in harmony with the movements of the earth. These beautiful ideals have often been misinterpreted and grossly misused in dance. Modern dance has often been thought of as young girls imitating the blooming of a flower. Contrary to popular belief, Miss Duncan never improvised on stage and personally supervised every detail of her performances. Her great contributions are in three areas.

First, she began the expansion of the kinds of movements that could be used in dance. Before Miss Duncan danced, ballet was the only type of dance performed in concert. In the ballet the feet and legs were emphasized, with virtuosity shown by complicated, codified positions and movements. Isadora performed dance by using all her body in the freest possible way, taking her inspiration from the ancient Greek. She did not develop a technique as we know it today. Her dance stemmed from her soul and spirit. She was one of the pioneers who broke tradition so others might be able to develop the art.

Her second contribution lies in dance costume. She discarded corset, ballet shoes, and stiff costumes. These were replaced with flowing Grecian tunics, bare feet, and unbound hair. She believed in the natural body being allowed to move freely, and her dress displayed this ideal.

Her third contribution was in the use of music. In her performances she used the symphonies of great masters, including Beethoven and Wagner, which was not the usual custom.

She was as exciting and eccentric in her personal life as in her dance. Her two beautiful, illegitimate children who were tragically drowned, her many loves, and her death by strangulation from a long trailing scarf that accidentally wrapped around the wheel of a sports car—all these symbolize her dramatic life. She threw away the conventions which characterized the time in which she lived, 1878-1927. She has been portrayed in the film, *The Loves of Isadora*, and the dancing in this film is a near duplication of the way Miss Duncan moved.

Ruth St. Denis   While Isadora Duncan had looked to the West and classical Greece for inspiration in her new dance, Ruth St. Denis had looked to the East and the Orient to discover a new movement form. In 1906 she performed *Radha*, a dance which used an Oriental theme to communicate a spiritual message. It was so significant that it continued to be performed even in the 1940s when Miss Ruth was in her sixties. She was interested not just in virtuosity in dance but in communicating an idea. She did not develop a technique. Instead she believed music was to be "visualized" in order to produce dance movements.

In the scheme of the development of modern dance, Ruth St. Denis holds a vital position. She not only made specific contributions of her own but also provided, through the Denishawn Company, a proving ground for the next generation of dancers, including Martha Graham, Doris Humphrey, and Charles Weidman. Denishawn, which was a partnership and a marriage between Miss Ruth and Ted Shawn, proved successful for some sixteen years. During these years Denishawn was financially self-supporting, a unique position in the history of modern dance companies. Ruth St. Denis died in 1968.

Ted Shawn

Ted Shawn was co-director of Denishawn, and if Miss Ruth was its spirit, he was its form. He performed and choreographed in Denishawn until it dissolved. In the early 1930s he formed a company of male dancers who were ex-athletes. He taught baseball, football, and basketball players, wrestlers, and track stars dances with strong masculine themes such as *Olympiad* and *Labor Symphony*. Through his efforts, he helped to raise the status of the male dancer in the United States by choreographing themes that promoted the masculine characteristics of the dancers.

Another major contribution to the dance world by Ted Shawn has been the initiation of the Jacob's Pillow center in Massachusetts. This is a residence for dancers where they may study and perform. A festival is held there late each summer where works are presented in concert.

Mary Wigman

Isadora Duncan is considered to be in the first generation of modern dance, and the Denishawn Company is considered to be in the second generation. Mary Wigman, who came from the German School of modern dance, is also considered to be in the second generation. Wigman was regarded as the genius and the leader of German modern dance from 1924. She studied dance with Dalcroze (whose full name was Émile Jaques-Dalcroze and who created a way to teach the coordination of music and body movements called eurythmics) and with Rudolf Laban (who developed one of the methods of recording body movements on paper, which is now called Labanotation). She made many contributions to the development of modern

The Dancer Prepares

Isadora Duncan

Ruth St. Denis

Ted Shawn

dance. For instance, since movement is the substance of dance, dance should be movement alone; therefore, she composed dance without music so that movement would be stressed. She explored fully the use of space. She visited the United States in the early 1930s and again in 1964. Her pupil, Hanya Holm, adapted the German modern dance to American dancers' needs and characteristics.

Martha Graham   Probably the most exacting technique and the greatest number of choreographic works have come from Martha Graham. Her technique is built on the breathing cycle of the body and its principle of "contraction and release." (Other principles developed by her are called "motor memory" and "percussive movement.") In brief, Graham's dance is built on the process of inhaling and exhaling. She believes that in inhaling the body has an aerial quality of release, and in exhaling the body "drive has gone down and out" in contraction. Almost all of today's dancers,

Doris Humphrey and Charles Weidman

Martha Graham

Mary Wigman

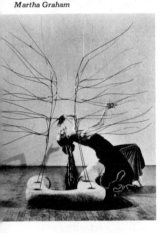

Merce Cunningham

GERDA PETERICH

Alwin Nikolais

BASIL LANGTON

choreographers, and modern dance classes have been influenced by her technique.

Another major contribution by Miss Graham has been in the area of choreography and performance. She has been considered one of the finest dance concert performers. She utilizes the wide spectrum of life in the themes of her outstanding works. She often uses themes from Greek drama to symbolize and probe the inner man. Her dance company has included some of the outstanding dancers in the world.

Martha Graham and Doris Humphrey both left Denishawn, and each established her own school. Both developed theories and philosophies of movement that are significant to the growth of modern dance, and both are considered to be in the art's third generation.

Doris Humphrey

Doris Humphrey was a protégé of Ruth St. Denis and her movements were of the same lyrical quality. She built her dance principles on the "fall-recovery" theory which she created. She believed dance movement came about by periods of unbalance and balance in the body. She stated that "fall-recovery" consisted of three separate movements: the *fall,* the *recovery* from the fall, and the *suspension* held at the peak of recovery. She also perfected compositions using large-scale dramatic themes for groups of dancers.

Charles Weidman

She formed an alliance with Charles Weidman, who had also been in the Denishawn Company. Mr. Weidman is known for his biting, satirical dance works and his skill as a male performer. Together they formed one branch of American modern dance. Miss Humphrey performed her works until 1945, when crippling arthritis ended her performing career. She continued choreographing and working until her death in 1958. Some of her most brilliant works from 1945 on were created for José Limón, an important choreographer in his own right.

Merce Cunningham

The present generation of dancers has either directly or indirectly studied with the pioneers of modern dance. Of the dancers working in the 1960s, Merce Cunningham has stirred the most controversy with his works. Mr. Cunningham choreographs "by chance," holding to the idea that "any movement can follow any other movement." Regarded as avant-garde, he has choreographed and performed works which audiences either adore or abhor, depending upon their individual convictions. His admirers point to his fine artistic sense, his intelligence, and his superb company as factors which make the works he creates brilliant movement pieces.

Alwin Nikolais

Alwin Nikolais is another fourth generation American modern dance choreographer. His contribution has been in the creation of a form of theater which includes props, costumes, films, slides, sound, and light as extensions of the bodies of the dancers. His visual effects and illusions often remind the audience of events in their own experience, yet the works contain no story or conventional plot. The dancers' bodies are often distorted or hidden in the costumes and props to emphasize Nikolais' abstract images and suggestions.

Serge Diaghileff

Michel Fokine

Although modern dance in its infancy disregarded and rejected ballet, all ballet did not reject similar changes in dance. The Diaghileff Ballet, under the powerful artistic direction of Serge Diaghileff, flourished from 1909 to 1929 in London and Paris and fostered many choreographers. One, the genius Michel Fokine, changed ballet radically with his five cardinal rules for ballet, developed independently from the modern dance movement. He believed all the elements of a ballet—costumes, combinations of steps, sets, etc.—should contribute to the central idea of the choreographer. He believed the style and flavor of the ballet should be in keeping with the locale and time from which it came. These were radical departures from accepted ballet, which until Fokine's time had usually used a recurring combination of steps and styles of costumes and sets, regardless of the theme of the ballet. Fokine was followed by Vaslav Nijinsky, the brilliant dancer, who became a choreographer for Diaghileff. Nijinsky choreographed the controversial and very modern *The Rite of Spring* with music by Igor Stravinsky. This work, which used parallel feet positions, noncodified movements, unconventional costumes, and unusual new music, created so much opposition that spectators actually fought in the aisles of the concert hall on opening night in Paris in 1913.

Vaslav Nijinsky

Later American ballet choreographers were to incorporate modern dance movements into their ballets. In the Fokine tradition, the American choreographer Eugene Loring incorporated modern movements into his ballet *Billy the Kid* in 1938. Agnes De Mille called this work "the first authentic American masterpiece," and it still stands as one of the finest ballets using a native American theme and movements peculiar to the old American West. An endless list of choreographers have since made exciting contributions to the growth and development of a unique American dance idiom. The keynote of their work is its infinite variety—from George Balanchine to Jerome Robbins to Gower Champion to Alvin Ailey to Peter Gennaro.

Eugene Loring

As dancers and choreographers explore new ways of moving and create more relevant means of communication with the audience, modern dance changes, incorporates, and adopts these new ideas. The difference between the pioneers and the dancers of today is that today's dancers have a strong, proven foundation from which to work. Modern dance has only one predictable characteristic: it is always changing and growing. This is the trait that makes it exciting and significant.

"Each dance is unique and free, a separate organism whose form is self-determined."

—Mary Wigman

CHAPTER 6

Choreographic Approaches

Some students ask, "Why should I study choreography when all I want to do is dance?" It's true that a brilliant dancer may never have choreographed anything, and a brilliant choreographer may have been a poor dancer. A successful performer, however, doesn't just dance. He dances about something or to express something, even when the dance is without a plot. If you hope to make a statement with your body that reflects your intentions or the choreographer's, you should have some idea of the choreographic structure behind the dance you are doing. If you want to teach dancing or choreograph someday, then you can save yourself countless hours of aimless experimentation by knowing a few techniques of how to begin your experiments.

Improvisation and basic choreographic forms should be as much a part of your training as daily technique classes. Technique classes train the body. Improvisation frees your movement from the restrictions placed on it by a codified technique and frees your own creative energies. Knowledge of choreographic structures trains your mind and sharpens your critical faculties and perceptions.

There are many ways to choreograph. You will find the way that works best for you. We have presented here only a few basic approaches to choreographic exploration.

DESIGN
48

A sense of body design in space and good stage balance comes with experience. There are a number of things you can do to help develop your "artistic eye" for line, form shape, and theatrical drama.

Pictures are telegraphic. They tell you a story without the addition of a caption below them. Dance should be able to do the same. Try the following exercises to help develop your artistic eye: (1) Look at paintings of different periods of history. Observe how the artist has placed the people in relationship to one another, how the people are posed, and why their clothes make them stand out the way they do. (2) Study the pictures in a pictorial magazine like *Life* and see why some pictures and advertisements make you want to look at them. (3) Look at the pictures of athletes in "frozen" motion and trace the natural lines of their movement. (4) Look at the buildings or the landscape around you and ask what is beautiful or ugly about it.

Observing Design

Study people and nature. If you want to dance about people and their universal concerns, you have to understand them and what makes them behave as they do in a given set of circumstances. (1) Watch how people of different ages and social classes walk, sit, and stand. (2) Observe how people move when they are happy, sad, or expressing some emotion. (3) Watch how people in a social situation group themselves into a circle or how some sit off by themselves. (4) Watch how children, animals, and birds move and consider why they move that way. (5) Study the shapes formed by a tree, a leaf, a rock, or oil stains on a mud puddle.

All of life, all of nature, is potentially the concern of the artist; he must bring some kind of order out of the myriad possibilities through selection and emphasis.

There are two basic modes of stage design: symmetrical and asymmetrical. In symmetrical design the stage is equally balanced on all sides. For example, if you have two dancers on one side of the stage, then you have two dancers on the other side. In asymmetrical design, the stage is not balanced. If you have two dancers on one side of the stage, you might have four on the other side in staggered positions. Symmetrical design is the most pleasing to look at; therefore it becomes the most dull to look at if overused.

Two Kinds of Design

Presumably you are choreographing for an audience, so you want to keep their eyes constantly "entertained" with unexpected movements, lines, shapes, and forms. There is nothing worse than putting your audience to sleep. There are no bad audiences—only bad dancers and choreographers. You have a responsibility to communicate something to a paying audience even if it is outraged at what you have done. The worst thing you can do to your audience is cause indifference or boredom, unless that is your intention.

IMPROVISATION

One of the best ways to find new movement is to get up and move around as freely as you can, with no planning whatsoever. In order to improvise successfully, you have to let yourself go completely, without any sense of embarrassment and without any awareness of the other class members watching you. Complete freedom of movement should be your goal. If music is played, then try to move with the mood of the music.

Totally free improvisation of this kind is not always easy or desirable in the beginning, so it is probably better to work with some limited but clearly defined plan. The improvisational possibilities below are a beginning for further exploration. Use the whole body or parts of the body in the movements.

Use of Space

Limit yourself to two or three basic spatial patterns and move only in those areas. For example: (1) While standing in one place, make all your movements straight up, straight down, or out at right angles to the body. (2) While walking in a square or on straight lines (no curved lines), make movements that are around the axis of your body near the knees or over the head.

Use of Time

To improvise by using time, you may do a set movement at varying speeds. For example, start slowly with some predetermined movement pattern, increase the speed of it until the movement is extremely fast, and then reverse the procedure.

Use of Qualities

Select one or more qualities and set up some kind of restrictions on their use. For example: (1) Start with a small swing, increase the arc of succeeding swings until the whole body is involved (crescendo), and then reverse the swings until they get smaller (decrescendo). (2) Alternate percussive and suspended movements. First do eight counts of each, then four of each, then two of each, then one of each.

Emotions, Ideas, Images, and Atmosphere

Emotions, ideas, images, and atmosphere can be used separately or together, or they can be combined with other approaches. Here are examples of their use together: (1) While walking through a park on a warm spring day, express the joy you feel in movement, then at some point become aware of the clouds that soon release a shower of rain on you and your best clothes. (2) Imagine yourself in a brightly lit room. Suddenly the lights go out; you hear strange noises that you finally realize are made by the walls closing in on you; the walls keep closing in on you until they have forced you into a tiny ball on the floor. Express your reactions to these events with movements as exaggerated as you can make them.

Another approach to finding new movement or to defining a character in a dance work is to improvise from human stereotypes, from the psychological make-up of a specific person, from gestures or common movement activities like throwing a ball, or by using an animal as a reference point for character definition.

If you are going to choreograph a part—a swaggering braggart, for example—you could ask yourself such questions as what motivates this person, what does he want, and how does he move. An easy way to begin is to decide that he acts like some animal, maybe a strutting rooster. You could then improvise around the idea of a rooster strutting with his chest pushed forward and his head quickly surveying all of his domain.

Gesture

Another approach to defining his character with movement is to improvise on some imaginary situation he might be in. For example, if he were in a room full of people and was offered food, how would he take the food from a tray and how would he eat it?

If the movement is to be repeated and set into a dance for the character, it is helpful to decide first on a few extreme examples of what this person moves like, or extreme static poses that he might assume, then combine them together, moving from static positions or from movement pattern to movement pattern. You can eventually arrive at specific movements that get your idea across. The tendency with novice choreographers is to put everything they know indiscriminately into the dance. An audience will probably see the choreography only once and so must be carefully led to see the idea that you want them to see.

Abstraction of Character

You will not always choreograph or dance as a literal, recognizable character, but as an abstraction of an idea or character. These same methods of choreographic improvisation and definition can be utilized until you have arrived at the essence of what you wanted to say in movement. For example, if you pick a flower from a garden, you could go through the actual motions of picking a flower (literal gesture) or a stylized motion of picking a flower (pantomime) or an extended motion suggesting the picking of a flower, indicating the joy or nostalgia you feel, rather than the actual picking of the flower (dance).

FORMS

Many people have ideas but lack the ability to share them with others. That is why you as a choreographer or dancer have to develop the craft of organizing your ideas into some structure that will communicate them to the audience.

There is no easy formula that will guarantee success, but a few forms that you can organize your ideas around are presented here as possibilities to start with. (Some of these basic forms require more than one dancer.)

Theme

The theme is one of the most elemental forms. It is particularly useful when you begin to choreograph extended pieces. A theme makes some basic statement and is organized around some central movement idea. For example, using the idea of a "work theme" you could choreograph a movement pattern of eight bars suggesting the movements of a lumberman chopping down a tree. The movement theme: he chops the tree.

Theme and Variation

The basic movement theme is shown once, then repeated with some kind of basic change. The common ways of doing the variation are: (1) Slowing down or (2) speeding up the entire movement pattern; (3) inverting the movement (for example, movements that go up now go down, movements that came toward the body now go away from the body); (4) reversing the movement pattern (that is, starting at the end and working toward the beginning); (5) extending the amount of time selected movements are performed or (6) diminishing the amount of time selected movements are performed; and (7) embellishing or adding movement to the basic theme or (8) eliminating movement from the basic theme.

Starting with the basic chopping theme, then doing each of these eight variations for eight bars, you would end up with a choreographic piece that was seventy-two bars long. In embellishing the basic theme you might add the idea that the lumberman stops to wipe his brow with a handkerchief because of the heat or he stops to sharpen the cutting blade or to watch the tree fall.

By combining the basic theme with variations or with some other form, you can tell a story or suggest a change of mood or anything that you want to communicate, and

yet beneath it all is a basic structure that has a unity
with your basic premise, the original eight bars of movement.

The fugue requires more than one dancer. For example, *Fugue*
you start with the basic theme of chopping for eight bars.
This original eight bars is repeated exactly the same way
by the same dancer or other dancers throughout the entire piece, while the original dancer or some other danc-
er(s) does variations on the original theme.

The sonata form is made up of two themes, primary *Sonata*
and secondary, plus a recapitulation or joining of the two
themes. For example, in theme one the man chops the
tree. In theme two the man watches the tree fall. In the
recapitulation the man again chops the tree and watches
it fall. In such a recapitulation of the two themes you
might have the idea of felling a forest and not merely one
tree.

The round is a common form exemplified by the song *Round*
"Three Blind Mice." The same theme is repeated a number of times with new dancers joining in at some point.
The beginning dancer finishes first, then the other dancers
stop as they finish the same movement pattern. For example, (movement A) The man chops the tree, (movement B) the man wipes his brow, and (movement C)
the man watches the tree fall. In a simple round the first
dancer(s) starts at movement A, continues through movements B and C, and stops. The second dancer(s) begins
at movement A when the first dancer begins movement B
and continues to the end and stops. The third dancer(s)
begins movement A when the second dancer begins at
movement B and continues to the end and stops. The first
dancer, instead of stopping at the end of movement C,
may introduce new movement themes which are repeated
by the second and third dancer.

The canon form is similar to the round except that all *Canon*
the dancers finally join in the same movement to bring
it to an end (coda). In dance canon, each new dancer
does the movement exactly as the original movement was
done, but the new dancer may be a different physical or
emotional type from the original dancer. In the original
theme the lumberman chops the tree. In the successive
repeats of the theme he may be joined by his wife and
then by his son.

In counterpoint two independent themes are danced *Counterpoint* against one another. The lumberman chops the tree while someone builds a house using the material the lumberman has produced.

Chance Composition

Choreography by chance is here called a form because the artist must still select and shape the final piece. A common example might be your placing a certain number of movement instructions written on individual pieces of paper into a box, then drawing them out one at a time and assembling them into a movement pattern in the same order you drew them out. For example, you might draw out these instructions (1) move in a circle, (2) make percussive movements, and (3) exhale. Using the idea of the lumberman, you might have him circle the tree, chop it sharply, and exhale with fatigue. It should be understood, however, that choreography by chance usually implies the lack of a preconceived theme.

All of these forms could, of course, be built around some other theme—abstract, literal, or movement-oriented.

MUSIC

Music can add a great deal to your choreography or it can destroy it. There are a few things to keep in mind when you are working with music. (However, you might want to choreograph the dance in *opposition* to these ideas in order to achieve a dissonant look in your movement.) (1) Keep the qualities of the dance movement consistent with the mood of the music (or, for contrast, deliberately work against the mood of the music). (2) Analyze the structure of the music so that you can repeat the movements on the same counts or phrases twice running or so that you can teach the movement to someone else without being vague about what happens when. A pencil and paper are invaluable. Make dashes on the paper in accompaniment with the regular beats of the music until you have developed some kind of musical pattern to work from. As you listen over and over to the music, make notes above the dashes to indicate shifts in the rhythm, shifts in the mood, or new instruments entering—or make whatever other notes can guide you. (3) Try composing your own music. You might play it *while you are dancing* or have someone play it for you. You can use percussion instruments if they are available. If not, so much the better: find and use rocks, sticks, or dried leaves on a branch. Or run a comb over paper. You can discover exciting new sounds by trying out the unlikeliest objects. Then organize the sounds into some repeatable form. If you have access to a tape recorder, you can record your music. A tape recorder makes it possible to use other sounds as well, like a ticking clock, an airplane, dripping water, or a cat's cry. Composing your own music frees you from the restrictions placed on you by the composer, and can be a lot of fun as well.

COSTUMES, PROPS, AND SCENERY

If you are going to wear a costume or use scenery and props, take advantage of them by analyzing their function in relation to your purposes. For example, if you are wearing a long cape, experiment to find out how many different ways you can move it or use it to augment the spatial designs of your body. Can it be used as a prop like a bullfighter's cape or placed on the floor to suggest a forbidden territory that no one dares enter? The important thing to remember about a dance costume is that you don't just wear it, you take advantage of its restrictions and use them to enhance your visual designs or enhance your ideas.

Costumes do not need to be expensive in order to be effective. Using your leotards and tights as a basic costume, you can perform wonders with pieces of unsewn material or dyes.

If you use stage props, explore all their possibilities. For example, an ordinary chair can be sat on, lain on, stood on, crawled under or over, or danced with like a silent partner. The list is endless.

Costumes, props, and scenery make it possible to extend the potentials of your body design in space and to add new elements of stage interest. The only limitations to movement possibilities are those that come from your not being imaginative or from your deliberately being selective.

If you become discouraged in your experiments, keep in mind that even the most famous of choreographers started at the beginning. No less than they, you have to work at your craft if you want eventually to use it to express your ideas and feelings.

> *"We have to meet the artist halfway. We have to bring something before we can bring something away."*
>
> —Clive Barnes

CHAPTER 7

Evaluation Techniques

Often you hear people say of something they have seen, "I liked it," or "I didn't like it." This is the beginning of criticism. Unfortunately most people never go beyond these statements to analyze why they "liked" or "didn't like" what they saw.

If you want to dance, choreograph, teach, or be an intelligent member of the audience, it is important to you that you know why you "liked" or "didn't like" something and be able to express your viewpoint intelligently. You can learn a great deal of what to do and what not to do in the dance theater by seeing dance concerts and by critically evaluating what you have seen. Your criticisms should never be exclusively negative or positive. You should impartially evaluate both the good and the bad features.

You may not be able to see dance concerts regularly, but you can increase your critical faculties and perceptions in other ways. Every movie, television show, advertisement, short story, etc., has a structure and makes a statement in some way—good or bad. You can apply the same principles to these communication forms that you do to dance.

You can analyze the structure by asking yourself how it began, how it ended, and what happened in between. A well-structured dance should have a beginning, a development of the beginning, and a resolution. The form may or may not be used to tell a story. Nevertheless, it should start somewhere, accomplish something, and be resolved.

Next you can ask yourself how the choreographer handled the individual parts of the structure. (1) Did the music and the dance complement one another in an effective way? (2) Were the costumes, props, and scenery related to the theme, and were they effectively utilized? (3) Were the individual movements and movement patterns original, visually interesting, right for the idea being expressed, as well as being logically related to the whole work? (4) With a professional company you have the right to ask if the work was performed well and if the dancers contributed to the choreographer's conception. Many good works are ruined by bad dancers, and many bad works are effective when performed by good dancers. (5) Was it theatrically exciting? There is no law that says art cannot be entertaining. The audience has a right to expect something more for its time and money than a pedestrian presentation of an idea.

If you decide you liked the concert, ask yourself "Why did I like it?" Because it was a good story well told? Because the costumes, music, and lights were enchanting? Because the dancing was exciting? Was it a combination of all three? Was it something else?

If you didn't like it, ask yourself first if you came with a preconception of what dance is supposed to be, and this company didn't live up to your idea. If you want to develop your critical abilities and sensibilities, you have to be open to new ideas and new approaches in dance. Remember that many of the dance movements of the modern dance pioneers were thought strange and ugly by an audience unaccustomed to this new way of moving. You don't have to accept as "great" everything you see, but you should know why you consider something great, mediocre, or merely pleasing.

Like the muscles of your body, your critical faculties and perceptions are developed by being used regularly. Incorrect training makes muscles that are undesirably bulky. In a similar way, a closed mind impedes your creativity and stops the flow of new ideas in your evaluations and in your own work.

Selected References

PREPARATION

De Mille, Agnes. *To a Young Dancer.* Boston and Toronto: Little, Brown and Co., 1962.

Gilbert, Pia and Aileene Lockhart. *Music for the Modern Dance.* Dubuque, Iowa: Wm. C. Brown Co., 1961.

ANATOMY

First Aid, American Red Cross.

Gelabert, Raoul. *Anatomy for the Dancer.* 2 vols. New York: Dance Magazine, 1964 and 1966.

Wells, Katharine F. *Kinesiology.* 4th ed. Philadelphia: W. B. Saunders Co., 1966.

HISTORY

Martin, John. *Introduction to the Dance.* New York: Dance Horizons, 1965.

Maynard, Olga. *American Modern Dancers: The Pioneers.* Boston: Little, Brown and Co. 1965.

Terry, Walter. *The Dance in America.* New York: Harper & Row, 1956.

CHOREOGRAPHY

Ellfeldt, Lois. *A Primer for Choreographers.* Palo Alto, California: National Press Books, 1967.

Hawkins, Alma M. *Creating through Dance.* Englewood Cliffs, N.J.: Prentice-Hall, Inc., 1959.

Humphrey, Doris. *The Art of Making Dances.* New York: Grove Press, 1959.

EVALUATION AND CRITICISM

Van Praagh, Peggy and Peter Brinson. *The Choreographic Art.* New York: Alfred A. Knopf, 1963.

MAGAZINES

Dance Magazine (published monthly). 268 West 47th Street, New York, New York 10036

Dance Perspectives (published quarterly). 29 East 9th Street, New York, New York 10003

FILMS

Dance: Four Pioneers (Martha Graham, Doris Humphrey, Charles Weidman, Hanya Holm), National Educational Television.

Dance: Robert Joffrey Ballet (a brief look at a modern ballet company at work), National Educational Television.

A Dancer's World (Martha Graham and her company illustrate her philosophy), McGraw-Hill Text-Film Division, New York.

Night Journey (Martha Graham), University of California Extension Media Center, Berkeley, California.

Procession: Contemporary Directions in American Dance, University of California Extension Media Center, Berkeley, California.

Totem (Alwin Nikolais), Grove Press Film Division, New York.